INTRODUCTION TO THE MASTER TUTORIAL CLASSES

Hello and welcome. Once you understand how to operate the basics of chat g p T, you'll be able to overcome a blank screen when you need to produce content or you need to produce elements in your business that would otherwise be difficult to construct from scratch. At the same time, you must realize chat GPTs limitations. It does generate incorrect information. It also might produce information or lines or content that may be harmful to your brand or harmful in general.

It also is limited to the content that was on the internet. Now, as of the recording of this video chat, g p t is limited to the world in events as of 2021. That could change by the time you are looking at this video. Regardless, there are limitations, and so in your production of artifacts for your business, you're going to want focus on accuracy and citation when you can.

But chat G P T will help you to overcome a blank screen, and that is what we will do in this course is to undertake the writing of a sales presentation of an information product that you have created. Now, this will not take the place of a personal sales letter, nor will it take the place of a professional copywriter. What it will do is to help you if you have a blank screen in front of you.

And so we will start undertaking this process in the next video and in this course. Okay? So with that, thanks and I will see you in another chapter.

- Introduction to the Master Tutorial Classes
- ChatGPT: Conversation and Conventions
- Google Talks to book
- ChatGPT-Workaround for up to date statistical information
- Choosing a sales letter framework
- Ask for image prompts
- Canva Text to image for ChatGPT sales presentation
- Use ChatGPT to write headlines and sub headlines
- ChatGPT-Thank you page script
- Launch email to customers
- Launch email to affiliates
- ChatGPT- Script for the sales video
- AI with PowerPoint presentation coach
- AI with the powerpoint design and accessibility
- ChatGPT- Write a welcome email
- ChatGPT- Suggest a layout and order of the sales page
- ChatGPT- Suggest color and background of the sales page
- ChatGPT- Earning Disclaimers
- ChatGPT- Create the copy of the opt-in page
- Create an opt-in email with sales message
- Top 40 ways to make money with ChatGPT.
- Get the url to watch videos

CHATGPT: CONVERSATION AND CONVENTIONS

Welcome back. You're going to notice conversations on the left side menu that you had previously with the chatbot. You're also going to notice here at the top that there's a message from Chat G p T that says that they are experiencing high demand. With those two things combined, it is possible that this information that you see saved on the left side menu could be lost.

It could be lost due to the high demand. It could be lost due to challenges they may be having on their server. And so you want to make sure that you are saving as you go. And since we are going to use one conversation thread in order to produce a final document, we're going to undertake this process and we're going to use the words final draft whenever we can to indicate that when we want chat g p t to go back and to get information to produce a final document.

We want to produce information from this individual chat with these words as we have written them. So we are writing these words as a signal when we can, and we will do that throughout the production of this document. Now, before we start the process of a sales presentation, we do want to do some background research, and we're actually going to do that with an AI outside of chat G P T, and we're going to do that with Google Talk to books, and we will do that in the next video. Okay? So with that, thanks and I will see you in the next chapter.

GOOGLE TALKS
TO BOOK

Welcome back. Now, one background information tool that you may want to use that does not exist inside of chat. G p t is called Google Talk to books. And if you go to your favorite search engine, you're going to see here that there is a link called Talk to Books from Google Books. And we're going to click on that link. And talk to books is a semantic search tool from Google accessing the words inside of published books on Google Books.

So we're going to write in a semantic search term. Once we have our phrase, we are then going to click go. And what you will have is direct citations from specific books regarding your query. Now you can go back and redo your query if you don't get the results that you like. What you get with this page also is a filter command and we can click on filter.

And if you have a way of filtering the information, you can do so here in this area we can view more passages for more books. And again, these are books that we are going to cite directly in sight of whatever artifact that we are producing. And in some cases we may even link back to the book either with an affiliate link, but definitely with some kind of credit to the author.

What this also does is it allows us to verify that what we are stating in our artifact is going to be correct and accurate. So you can use the AI in Google, talk to books in order to find background information and direct citation information. Okay? So with that, thanks and I will see you in another lesson.

CHATGPT-WORKAROUND FOR UP TO DATE STATISTICAL INFORMATION

Welcome back. Now chat. G p t is unable to get statistical information from specific websites and when we are seeking statistical information, we're going to need to work around the fact that their statistics are typically going to be lagging behind the point at which you are going to be producing the artifact, requiring numerical or statistical information. If you are willing to abide by the terms of service and to cite the authors, you can use websites such as staa and in some cases some of these statistical information is available for use in your projects without having a paid account. And depending on your topic, you are going to see a considerable amount of information that you may find useful in your sales presentation.

A similar site where you can gain this kind of information as well as to pro, as well as to be provided. A visual chart is going to be the website marketing charts.com. And again, depending on your topic, you will be able to find updated information that you can use in your sales presentation along with the visual chart to make the point inside of your content. Now, obviously there are niche based statistical tools that you can use to work around chat gpts, inability to go beyond a certain point in time. So you will want to make sure that you have updated statistics with sites like the two that were mentioned as well as similar sites. Okay? So with that, thanks and I will see you in another lesson.

CHOOSING A SALES LETTER FRAMEWORK

Welcome back. One of the things that we can do in doing a sales presentation is we can ask chat g p t what the best frameworks are for writing sales letters. And so we're going to do that right now and we're going to ask a specific question and we're going to ask the chatbot to list 10 frameworks. And once we have our information in, we're then going to click enter. Once you have your frameworks, one of the things that you can do based on the information that you already have in your conversation with chat g p t, is to ask the chatbot to use it as a context. And so that's what we're going to do right now. Going to ask the chat bot to use one of the frameworks to write a specific sales presentation.

And we're now going to click enter and we're going to allow chat g p T to do its work with the framework we've asked it to use for the above sales presentation. So once the process is complete, you're going to go through each framework and you're going to determine which of the frameworks you like best in order to work with in order to go forward.

Once we've chosen the framework, we're going to work with that framework in detail. Now, for some elements of a sales presentation, we're actually going to use other frameworks, and now that we have them listed in this conversation, we will then be able to use them. Now we're not yet ready to start creating for a final draft, so what we're going to do right now is we're going to move to the next step of adding in personalized and background information.

Okay? So with that, thanks, and I will see you in another lesson.

ASK FOR IMAGE PROMPTS

Welcome back. Now, one of the ways we can personalize or give life to the sales presentation that we're going to be using is to add images and we can add appropriate images as we see fit according to the context we're going to be communicating in. One of the other things that we can do with chat g p t is we can ask the chatbot what kind of images would be appropriate for this particular sales presentation, and we're going to do that right now. We're going to ask chat, g p t to tell us what kind of images would compliment this sales presentation. And so we're going to ask a playing language question, and we're now going to click enter. Now that we have ideas on what we're going to add as images, and we have a specific number, we're now going to go back to chat G p T, and we're going to ask it to give us prompts to place insight of an image creator. And so we're going to write the first query, knowing that we may need to rewrite the query until we get what it is that we want. So we're going to ask the chatbot to give us the prompt in order to create the images.

We're now going to click enter. Now what we're going to do with these prompts is we're going to take them and we're going to go to an image creator in order to create each of the images, and these are going to be the images that we will consider using in our sales presentation when we do the final layout after we get all of the content from chat G p T.

Okay? So with that, thanks, and I will see you in another lesson.

CANVA TEXT TO IMAGE FOR CHATGPT SALES PRESENTATION

Welcome back. You are now looking@canva.com and we're going to work within canva.com in order to create the images that we have has suggested to us by chat G P T. What you'll do first is to create a custom size image. You'll typically create a square image. You'll then create a design, which you'll then do, is to go to your apps area, and you're going to choose the text to image application. You're going to see it here on our left side panel, but you can choose it here from the new apps. What you're then going to do is you're going to place in the text from chat G p T, we're going to select one of the image prompts. Once we have our prompt, we're going to select photo.

We're going to then generate the image, and we can select an image that we want. We can add it, and typically what we can do here is we can then set the image at the background. What we can then do inside of Canva is we can download the image. So we're going to do here is we're going to click download and we're going to download the image as a p and g file, and we have now created an appropriate image to use in our sales presentation. Okay, with that, thanks, and I will see you in another lesson.

USE CHATGPT TO WRITE HEADLINES AND SUB HEADLINES

Welcome back. Now in the sales presentation, you are typically going to want to have specific headlines and the best headlines you can use at the top of your sales presentation. And you can use those that are not quite as good as sub headlines throughout your presentation. And so what you're going to want to do is to ask chat g p t to give you headlines to use in your presentation.

And so we are going to ask chat g p t to write five headlines. We're going to give the chatbot context. So we're now going to give chat g p t some specific parameters and we're now going to click enter. Now obviously we returned an error. So what we did was we pushed the F five button to refresh our page and we're going to give chat G p t another prompt to give us more information.

So we are going to alter the text slightly and we're going to click enter and we're now going to get our information. Now the machine did not quite understand our query, so what we're going to do is we're going to ask for five specific headlines and we're now going to hit enter. So now what we're going to do is we're going to ask chat g p T to rewrite our sales letter and to use our headlines and our sub-headlines.

And we're going to give chat G P T A suggestion answer. What we're going to now do is we're going to now ask the chat bot to write in a different voice for the final draft, and we're now going to click enter and we now have our next draft. Okay? So with that, thanks, and I will see you in another lesson.

CHATGPT-THANK YOU PAGE SCRIPT

Welcome back. We are now going to use chat G p t in order to help us to write a script for our thank you page. So we're going to include some additional elements and we're going to include the elements that we want the chatbot to consider. But once again, we are looking for information that we can use in order to help us with a blank page.

We may or may not use all of the information that chat g p t gives us, but we expect to be off to a good start with the information. So we are going to give the chatbot a prompt as is the case with anything you want chat g p t to do. The more information that you give it, the better the output it will give back to you.

But again, we are using all of the information that we have created inside of this conversation in order to help the chatbot with this process. So now that we have written out our instructions, we are now going to click enter. Now again, we may or may not like the full text that we receive back from the chatbot. Now in this case, we're going to ask the chatbot to rewrite this thank you page message, and we're going to make a change to it. So we've now added in some additional verbiage. We're now going to click enter. Now it's at this point that we may need to take the text as we have it, as our query isn't fully clear to the chatbot exactly what we want.

So we'll work with the first draft of the thank you page and make the adjustment ourselves. But basically you can give the chat bot instructions so that you can have information to keep you from having a blank page and you can make any necessary adjustments according to your context. Okay, with that, thanks and I will see you in another lesson.

LAUNCH EMAIL TO CUSTOMERS

Welcome back, just as you did for sales letters. It's a good idea to consider what are the best frameworks for writing sales emails to your customers. And so we're going to ask chat G p T that very same question. It's likely that you'll get the same information that you got for the sales letters, however, there may be different information that it can find when it scrapes the internet.

So again, we're going to give as specific a prompt as we can give it. We're then going to click enter. In this case, you'll notice that the information that we received is going to be slightly different from the information that we received in terms of a framework for a sales letter. And so based on this fact, we may choose one of the unique elements that we received from chat G P T in order to write our customer sales email.

And so we are going to take one of the frameworks and we're going to give the chatbot some additional information about writing the email. And we are now going to click enter. Now, in this case, the framework did not seem to help the chatbot to write a sufficient email. So in this case, we're just going to ask the chatbot to write an email selling the product.

And this time we're going to instruct the chatbot not to mention the price. We're now going to click enter. And in this case, we were able to get better output and so we have something to work with in terms of our initial email to our customers. What you can do with the context that you have, as long as you continue to keep a conversation about the same project, you will then be able to use all of the previous information in order to give you content starters for specific pieces of content. Okay? So with that, thanks and I will see you in another lesson.

LAUNCH EMAIL TO AFFILIATES

Welcome back. We're going to take all of the same context that we have generated within this one conversation in order to generate a content starter for a message to affiliate marketers to promote the product that is now being released. And so we're going to give the chatbot some context and we're going to ask it to write an email to our existing affiliates. So now to undertake this, we're going to make sure to give the chat bot as much context as we possibly can. Once we do that, we're going to click enter, and what we're looking to get is a content starter. Even if we choose not to use the entire email written to us by chat G p T, we're now going to click enter and we have been given an error message.

So what we're going to do is we're going to copy this information and we're going to hit the F five button and we're going to come back and we're going to try to rep paste the same information and we're going to hit enter to see if our query is going to be answered. So what you'll see is that you have a good content starter with good sales messaging that you can massage for your individual use to send your affiliates and that chat, g p t uses the context that we have created in the entire conversation. Okay? So with that, thanks and I will see you in another lesson.

CHATGPT- SCRIPT FOR THE SALES VIDEO

Welcome back. We are going to use the entire context we have created in order to write a sales video script. Now, in this case, what we're going to do is we're going to make sure to give the chatbot enough context to write the script for the sales video exactly the way we want it. What we're going to do is to produce a PowerPoint style sales script of about two minutes.

And so to do that we're going to give the chatbot a prompt and we're going to write the information in here. Once we've written in our detailed prompt, we're now going to click enter. Now we're going to ask chat g p t to rewrite the script. We're going to ask the, in order to write it in bullet point fashion, and we're going to ask the chat bot to write it for a longer period of time.

So we're going to work within the context and we're going to ask chat g p T in order to rewrite the script, and we're going to write it for a little longer. With this prompt, we're now going to click enter. Now you'll notice that the script is probably not five minutes long, and we might have to enter our own information in order to make it, but we do have a content starter. We have the information in all bullet points so that we can place it on our PowerPoint presentation. And we are now ready to begin writing our script for our sales video. Okay? So with that, thanks, and I will see you in another lesson.

AI WITH POWERPOINT PRESENTATION COACH

Welcome back. Now, if you are a user of PowerPoint, there are AI aspects that you can use in order to increase the effectiveness of your presentation When you begin to record your sales video, if you look inside of the slideshow tab, you're going to see an element here called Rehearse with Coach. You're going to click that link and basically this is going to allow you to rehearse your presentation, and you're going to see down on the right side area here, there's going to be an area here where you can start rehearsing. And basically when you click this button, you are going to narrate your presentation the way that you're actually going to do it, so that you can get feedback from PowerPoint telling you areas where you can improve. We're going to go ahead and we're going to click start Rehearsing, and we're going to narrate our presentation. Hey there, my name is Thomas Duncan, and I'm here to tell you that if you're tired of struggling to stand out on Facebook, that you're in the right place. I know what it's like, you're working hard, but you're not seeing the results you want. You're scrolling through your Facebook feed and you're thinking, why can't my business be more like that?

Now, I know you're busy and you don't have time for a course that takes forever to finish. That's why this course is easy to follow and you can implement strategies right away. That's not all. You'll also have access to incent support from me throughout and one-on-one help to ensure that you get the most out of the court. Okay? So what we're gonna do here is we're going to stop the presentation, and PowerPoint is going to give us an analysis of our presentation, and if we want, we can click rehearse again and we can rehearse the presentation again. So basically we're going to use the AI to give us suggestions on what we can do to increase the effectiveness of what it is that we are narrating. Okay? So with that, thanks and I will see you in another lesson.

AI WITH THE POWERPOINT DESIGN AND ACCESSIBILITY

Welcome back. Now, PowerPoint has two additional AI elements to its operation. One you'll find within the review tab, and you're going to see it here, that you can check accessibility to make sure that if you're going to be giving your presentation to someone in order to read that it is accessible to individuals that have accessibility issues. You can click here to check to make sure that there are no issues,and this means that your presentation is likely to be compliant with accessibility principles. Now the other AI element that you have available to you is in the home tab, and you're going to see it here in the right side, and you can open up what's called the designer, and that's going to open up the panel on the right side. And basically you're going to have an AI to give you suggestions on ways that you can put your slide together.

And you're going to have several choices for each slide. And basically you can choose one element for each slide, and each slide can be individually designed. But basically what you have available to you is that the AI will select different elements for you to determine how you want your slide presentation to look for any occasion that you will be using it for. Now, most cases a sales presentation will require just a plain background, but you may want to vary it depending on the context that you'll be selling your product. Okay? So with that, thanks and I will see you in another lesson.

CHATGPT- WRITE A WELCOME EMAIL

Welcome back. We are now going to use the entire existing context in order to write a welcome email for the customers that purchased the product. We're going to give chat G P T A prompt in order to undertake this task. Now, this first email, we are going to give chat G p t some instructions and we're going to tell the chat bot that this email is for one of the first 10 buyers,

which we have designated in a previous context that these individuals will receive a one-on-one consultation. And so now that we have all of our information in, we're now going to click enter and chat. G p t successfully wrote the email. That is a welcome email to one of the first 10 buyers. We are now going to ask the chat bot to write another email for those that purchase after the 10th buyer.

So we're going to give chat G p t another command. We're now going to click enter and chat g p t successfully left out the information for those that came after the 10th purchase so we can set this up inside of our autoresponder system to make sure that the right people get the right message. Okay? It's with that, thanks, and I will see you in another lesson.

CHATGPT- SUGGEST A LAYOUT AND ORDER OF THE SALES PAGE

Welcome back. We are now going to suggest a layout for the appearance of our sales letter. And in order to do that, we're going to give chat g p t some instructions in order to create the layout. We're going to write in our instructions. So what we've done is we are going to give chat g p t some additional instructions. We want the chat bot to give us a layout.

We want it to include the images that we have mentioned in this conversation. We wanted to position the sales video that we've mentioned in this conversation, and we also want to suggest an element that has not been mentioned in this conversation, which is the buy button or calls to action. Now that we have given the chatbot proper instructions, we're now going to click enter.

What we're now going to do is we're going to attempt to get chat G P T to rewrite the last sales letter in the context that it has just given us for the layout. So rather than ask the chatbot to remember, we're just going to cut and paste that same sales letter. We're going to ask it to suggest the same layout, but with the sales letter, it's already created. We're now going to click enter. So basically what chat G p T has done is it has given us a suggested layout. Now, obviously, we are going to have to make adjustments based on our own experience and what we think we need to do in order to sell to our customer. For example, the sales video is suggested near the end of the actual sales letter.

Typically, the sales letter is going to be closer to the beginning or sometimes at the very top. But you do have a starting point to begin your sales letter, and you have a suggestion on how it should be laid out and in the order in which the content should be placed, including the images. Okay? So with that, thanks and I will see you in another lesson.

CHATGPT- SUGGEST COLOR AND BACKGROUND OF THE SALES PAGE

Welcome back. Now that we have a proper layout for our sales page, one extra step that we can use chat g p t in order to help us with are the colors for our sales page. Now we may or may not get solid information, but we may get suggestions on the background color. We may be able to get suggestions on the color of our headlines.

We may be able to get suggestions for the color of our sub-headlines as well as our text. And so because of that we're going to go ahead and ask chat g p t for these suggestions. The first suggestions we're going to ask for is a background color. Now once again, we are talking to a machine and we are talking to a machine that has now context that we have been giving it in one conversation about one subject.

So now we're going to ask for a specific aspect of the layout. And so we are going to give it this prompt. We're now going to click enter and chat. G p T gives us a suggested background color, which we can test to determine if that's what we want to do. What we now want to do is we want to ask chat g P T for a suggested color for our headline as well as for our sub headlines.

And so we are going to give chat G P T A simple command and we're now going to click enter. And so we have suggestions for the background color. We have suggestions for our headline. And finally we want to have suggestions for the text of the actual letter. So we're going to write one more prompt to ask for that information and we're now going to click enter.

Now more than likely what we should have done with the prompt in suggesting colors for the main headline or sub-headlines is we should have specified that we wanted that information for the sales letter in the above layout. Again, we are talking to a machine and in some cases the machine may not know the full context even though we are still operating in one conversation within chat G P T.

So just for good measure, we are going to ask the question again, suggest colors separately for the main headline and sub-headlines for the above layout. Now that we have our request, we are now going to click enter and what we have proven with this response that chat g p t has given us is it actually did understand the context that we had given it when we ask for this information right above.

Okay? So with that, thanks and I will see you in another lesson.

CHATGPT- EARNING DISCLAIMERS

Welcome back. Now, depending on where you live in the world, you can ask Chat g p t to give you information on writing earnings disclaimers at essential pages. If you have a WordPress website, you can typically get these elements inside of certain plugins. However, if you choose not to operate using WordPress, you will want to have some kind of terms of service statement as well as an earnings disclosure.

Specifically when you're talking about a business related product. What we're going to do is assume that the business selling this product exists within the United States, and that we need to write an earnings disclaimer for this particular business and this particular product that we are selling. And we have our prompt. We are now going to click enter. Now, anything that you get from chat,

G P T should not be used in the place of legal advice. And so if you want to use this as a starting point, you still want to make sure that you are legally in compliance with laws in your country, in your region, and in your local area. Okay? So with that, thanks, and I will see you in another lesson.

CHATGPT- CREATE THE COPY OF THE OPT-IN PAGE

Welcome back. We are going to use the context we have created in order to write an opt-in page. And basically what we're going to do is we're going to give individuals information from one of the modules. Now we're going to ask chat g p t to write the copy for our opt-in page. So what we're going to do is we're going to paste in what the individuals are going to learn in the lead magnet.

We're going to paste that into the dialogue box, and then we're going to give the rest of the prompt and instructions to chat g p T. So we have written in our prompt and we have given the outline for the content in the lead magnet. So now what we're going to do is we're going to hit enter and chat. G p T is going to give us some output so you can use the entire context that you have created inside of the project in order to create an opt-in page.

And that's what we have done. Now, we don't have to use all of the content for this opt-in page, however, we are off to a good start with the content that chat G p t has given us. Okay, with that, thanks and I will see you in another lesson.

CREATE AN OPT-IN EMAIL WITH SALES MESSAGE

In conclusion, it's important to note that all of the assets that we have created in this course, we have created primarily with one Chat G P T conversation, and you'll see it here marked at the bottom on our left side menu. What we've done is we've leveraged this in getting responses with chat G P T to complete our entire project. We are now going to complete this project by writing an opt-in email for individuals that have received the free report, and then to remind them that there is a product that they can purchase that will help them beyond the scope of the lead magnet. We are going to give chat G p t the prompt in order to do it. So we are going to give several elements to the prompt and we're going to bring those elements in. And basically, now that we have the elements of our prompt, we are now going to click enter so that we can get our opt-in email. Now, one of the things you'll note about the opt-in email is that the chat bot remembered our support link. We didn't have to tell it what that support link is, and that has everything to do with us using the context we have created inside of one conversation. And so if you're going to be working with a specific project, it's a good idea to try to do all of that project in sight of one conversation. At the same time though, you wanna make sure that you're saving everything that you do since there is the possibility that Chat g p T could lose that information. Okay? So with that, thanks, and I'll see you either in another video, in another update or another course.

An Introduction to ChatGPT ChatGPT is a cutting-edge artificial intelligence language model developed by OpenAI. It's an advanced conversational AI system that can understand and respond to natural language input with human-like intelligence. ChatGPT is part of a growing trend in the AI industry, which aims to create machines that can understand and respond to human language in a more intuitive way. One of the key features of ChatGPT is its ability to generate coherent and informative text based on a given prompt. This makes it an incredibly versatile tool for a wide range of applications, from content creation and customer support, to virtual assistants and chatbots. The model is trained on a large corpus of text data, including news articles, books, and websites, which allows it to generate a wide range of responses based on the input it receives.

One of the main advantages of ChatGPT is its scalability. The model can be easily integrated into existing systems and workflows, allowing businesses and organizations to automate many of their language-based tasks. This can help companies save time and money, while also improving the accuracy and efficiency of their language-based processes.

Another benefit of ChatGPT is its ability to learn and adapt over time. As more and more data is fed into the model, it becomes better equipped to understand and respond to a wider range of input. This means that businesses can continually improve the quality and accuracy of their conversational AI systems, even as the complexity of their tasks increases. In addition to its technical capabilities, ChatGPT also offers a number of practical benefits for businesses and organizations. For example, it can be used to automate customer service, reducing the need for human agents and freeing up time for other tasks. It can also be used to generate personalized content and recommendations, helping businesses to build stronger relationships with their customers.

There are also many exciting applications for ChatGPT in the fields of education and entertainment. For example, the model can be used to generate educational content and materials, helping students to learn new concepts and skills in a more engaging and interactive way. It can also be used to generate interactive narratives and stories, providing new forms of entertainment for audiences. Despite its many benefits, there are also some challenges and limitations to using ChatGPT. One of the biggest challenges is ensuring the quality and accuracy of the model's outputs. This requires careful monitoring and quality control, as well as regular updates and maintenance. Additionally, there are also ethical concerns around the use of conversational AI, particularly when it comes to issues of privacy, transparency, and accountability.

In conclusion, ChatGPT is a powerful and versatile tool for businesses and organizations looking to automate their language-based tasks. Its ability to learn and adapt over time, as well as its scalability and ease of integration, make it an ideal solution for a wide range of applications. However, it is important to be aware of the challenges and limitations of using this technology, and to carefully consider the ethical implications of its use.

Can ChatGPT be used to make money?

Yes, ChatGPT can be used to make money. As a cutting-edge artificial intelligence language model, ChatGPT offers a wide range of opportunities for businesses and organizations to generate revenue through its use. One of the most straightforward ways to make money with ChatGPT is through content creation.

By using the model to generate articles, blog posts, and other forms of written content, businesses can save time and resources while also improving the quality and accuracy of their outputs. This can be especially useful for companies that produce large amounts of written content on a regular basis, such as news publishers, content marketing agencies, and e-commerce websites. Another way to make money with ChatGPT is through the creation of virtual assistants and chatbots. These conversational AI systems can automate many of the languagebased tasks associated with customer service, freeing up time for human agents to focus on more complex tasks. Additionally, ChatGPT-powered chatbots can provide 24/7 support for customers, improving the customer experience and boosting customer satisfaction. In addition to customer service, ChatGPT can also be used to generate personalized content and recommendations. For example, businesses can use the model to create virtual wine sommeliers, art advisors, and home decorators, which can provide customers with personalized recommendations based on their preferences and interests.

This not only improves the customer experience, but it can also drive sales and increase customer loyalty. Another potential source of revenue for businesses using ChatGPT is through the creation of educational and entertainment content. For example, the model can be used to generate interactive educational materials, such as quizzes, games, and simulations, which can be used in the classroom or for online learning. It can also be used to create engaging and interactive stories and narratives, which can be used for entertainment purposes. One of the key benefits of using ChatGPT to make money is its scalability. The model can be easily integrated into existing systems and workflows, allowing businesses to automate many of their language-based tasks with minimal effort.

Additionally, as more data is fed into the model, it becomes better equipped to understand and respond to a wider range of input, allowing businesses to continually improve the quality and accuracy of their conversational AI systems. Despite its many benefits, there are also some challenges and limitations to using ChatGPT to make money. One of the biggest challenges is ensuring the quality and accuracy of the model's outputs. This requires careful monitoring and quality control, as well as regular updates and maintenance. Additionally, there are also ethical concerns around the use of conversational AI, particularly when it comes to issues of privacy, transparency, and accountability. In conclusion, ChatGPT offers a wide range of opportunities for businesses and organizations looking to make money through the use of conversational AI.

Whether through content creation, virtual assistants, personalized recommendations, or educational and entertainment content, ChatGPT provides a scalable and flexible solution for businesses looking to automate their language-based tasks and generate revenue. However, it is important to be aware of the challenges and limitations associated with this technology, and to carefully consider the ethical implications of its use.

Here are some ways to use ChatGPT to make money: Customer Service Automation: Use ChatGPT to automate customer service queries and improve response times. This can reduce staffing costs and increase customer satisfaction. 40 Exciting Ways to Make Money With ChatGPT

1. Customer Service Automation: Use ChatGPT to automate customer service queries and improve response times. This can reduce staffing costs and increase customer satisfaction.

2. Content Generation: ChatGPT can be used to generate articles, blog posts, product descriptions, and other types of content. This can save time and reduce costs for content creation.

3. Chatbot Development: Develop and sell chatbots powered by ChatGPT for use in customer service, e-commerce, and other industries.

4. Language Translation: Use ChatGPT to generate high-quality translations for businesses, improving their global reach and competitiveness.

5. Lead Generation: Use ChatGPT to generate leads for businesses by automating lead-qualifying chat conversations.

6. Virtual Assistant: Offer virtual assistant services powered by ChatGPT to individuals or businesses, performing tasks such as scheduling, reminders, and information lookup.

7. Research Assistance: Use ChatGPT to assist with market research, data analysis, and other research tasks, providing valuable insights for businesses.

8. Sentiment Analysis: Use ChatGPT to perform sentiment analysis on customer feedback, social media posts, and other data sources, providing valuable insights for businesses.

9. Virtual Writing Assistant: Offer writing assistance services using ChatGPT to help with writing tasks such as editing, proofreading, and content generation.

10. Personal Shopping Assistant: Use ChatGPT to create a personal shopping assistant that helps customers find and purchase products online.

11. Virtual Tutor: Use ChatGPT to create a virtual tutor for students, providing personalized educational assistance and support.

12. AI Writing Coach: Offer writing coaching services using ChatGPT to help writers improve their writing skills and achieve their writing goals.

13. Virtual HR Assistant: Use ChatGPT to automate HR tasks such as interview scheduling, onboarding, and employee FAQs.

14. Virtual Therapist: Use ChatGPT to create a virtual therapy service that provides emotional support and counseling to individuals in need.

15. AI Creative Director: Use ChatGPT to generate creative ideas for advertising, marketing, and other creative projects.

16. Virtual Event Planner: Use ChatGPT to create a virtual event planning assistant that helps plan and organize events such as weddings, parties, and corporate events.

17. Virtual Career Coach: Use ChatGPT to create a virtual career coaching service that provides personalized career guidance and support.

18. AI Recruiter: Use ChatGPT to automate the recruitment process, including resume screening, candidate matching, and interview scheduling.

19. Virtual Travel Agent: Use ChatGPT to create a virtual travel agency that helps customers plan and book their travel itineraries.

20. Virtual Legal Assistant: Use ChatGPT to automate legal tasks such as document generation, contract review, and legal research.

21. AI Sales Assistant: Use ChatGPT to automate sales tasks such as lead generation, qualification, and follow-up.

22. Virtual Health Coach: Use ChatGPT to create a virtual health coaching service that provides personalized health and wellness advice.

23. Virtual Fitness Trainer: Use ChatGPT to create a virtual fitness training service that provides customized workout plans and fitness advice.

24. Virtual Nutritionist: Use ChatGPT to create a virtual nutrition service that provides personalized nutrition plans and healthy eating advice.

25. AI Stock Analyst: Use ChatGPT to generate stock market analysis and recommendations for individuals and financial

institutions.

26. Virtual Real Estate Agent: Use ChatGPT to create a virtual real estate agency that helps customers find and purchase properties.

27. Virtual Personal Stylist: Use ChatGPT to create a virtual personal styling service that provides personalized fashion advice and recommendations.

28. AI Event Speaker: Use ChatGPT to generate compelling speeches and presentations for events and conferences.

29. Virtual Personal Chef: Use ChatGPT to create a virtual personal chef service that provides customized meal plans and recipes.

30. Virtual Beauty Advisor: Use ChatGPT to create a virtual beauty advice service that provides personalized beauty and skincare recommendations.

31. AI Book Generator: Use ChatGPT to generate book outlines, plot summaries, and even complete novels for authors and publishers.

32. Virtual Art Advisor: Use ChatGPT to create a virtual art advisory service that provides personalized art recommendations and investment advice.

33. Virtual Pet Trainer: Use ChatGPT to create a virtual pet training service that provides customized training plans for pet owners.

34. AI Music Producer: Use ChatGPT to generate original music compositions, soundtracks, and beats for music producers and artists.

35. Virtual Wine Sommelier: Use ChatGPT to create a virtual wine tasting service that provides personalized wine recommendations and tasting notes.

36. AI Gift Finder: Use ChatGPT to create a virtual gift-finding service that helps customers find the perfect gift for any occasion.

37. Virtual Car Mechanic: Use ChatGPT to create a virtual car

repair service that provides troubleshooting advice and repair recommendations.

38. AI Gardening Coach: Use ChatGPT to create a virtual gardening service that provides personalized gardening advice and plant recommendations.

39. Virtual Home Decorator: Use ChatGPT to create a virtual home decorating service that provides personalized interior design recommendations.

40. AI Spiritual Coach: Use ChatGPT to create a virtual spiritual coaching service that provides personalized spiritual guidance and support.

How Can I Get Started With One Of The Ideas Above? Getting started with ChatGPT is relatively straightforward and can be done in the following steps:

• Familiarize yourself with the technology: ChatGPT is a large language model developed by OpenAI. Before you start using it, familiarize yourself with how it works and what it can do. Read about its capabilities and limitations, and learn about the architecture and training data used to build the model.

• Choose a platform: There are several platforms that provide access to ChatGPT, including OpenAI's own API, Hugging Face's Transformers library, and various cloud-based platforms like AWS, Google Cloud, and Microsoft Azure. Choose a platform that meets your needs and has the resources and support you need to get started.

• Get an API key: To use ChatGPT, you will need to get an API key from the platform you have chosen. This key will allow you to access the model and make requests to generate text.

• Integrate ChatGPT into your application: Depending on the platform you have chosen, there are different ways to integrate ChatGPT into your application. Some platforms provide pre-built libraries and SDKs that make it easy to get started, while others require more manual setup and integration.

• Test and fine-tune: Once you have integrated ChatGPT into your application, test it to make sure it is working as expected. You may need to fine-tune the model or adjust the parameters to get the results you want.

• Monitor and maintain: To ensure that ChatGPT continues to perform well, you will need to monitor its performance and make updates as needed. This may involve updating the model or the training data, or making other changes to the configuration or settings. By following these steps, you can get started with ChatGPT and start using it to generate text, answer questions, and perform other tasks. Keep in mind that ChatGPT is a complex technology, and you may need to invest time and resources to get the most out of it. But with the right tools and support, you can harness the power of ChatGPT to achieve your goals and make a real impact. What if I don't have the technical know-how to use one of the ideas above? If you're interested in outsourcing the creation of a ChatGPT AI, there are several steps you can follow to ensure a successful outcome:

• Define your requirements: Before you begin, take some time to define the scope of your project and what you want your ChatGPT AI to do. This will help you to determine what kind of resources you will need and what skills and expertise you will require from your outsourced team.

• Research potential vendors: There are a number of companies and freelancers who specialize in AI development, including ChatGPT. Research potential vendors to find those that have experience in creating conversational AI systems, and look for examples of their work to get a sense of their capabilities.

• Determine your budget: Knowing your budget will help you to narrow down your list of potential vendors and determine what you can afford. Be transparent about your budget constraints with the vendors you are considering so they can determine whether they can meet your needs within your budget.

• Evaluate the vendors: After you have a list of potential vendors, evaluate each one based on their skills, experience, portfolio, and price. This will help you to determine which vendor is the best fit for your project.

• Negotiate the terms: Once you have selected a vendor, negotiate the terms of the project. This includes the scope of the project, the budget, the timeline, and any other important details. Make sure that you have a clear understanding of what is included in the scope of the project and what is not.

• Manage the project: Once the project is underway, be proactive in managing it to ensure that it stays on track and that you get the results you want. This may involve regular check-ins with the vendor, providing feedback and guidance, and keeping track of the project timeline and budget.

• Ensure quality control: Finally, make sure that the final product meets your standards and requirements. Conduct thorough testing and quality control checks to ensure that the ChatGPT AI works as intended and that it is of high quality. By following these steps, you can outsource the creation of a ChatGPT AI with confidence, knowing that you have taken the necessary steps to ensure a successful outcome. Remember to be clear about your requirements, do your research, and manage the project effectively to ensure that you get the best results possible.

Note: Watch **CHATGPT** videos at https://www.youtube.com/@kalnews